Where Is
Broadway?

Where Is Broadway?

by Douglas Yacka and Francesco Sedita

illustrated by John Hinderliter

Penguin Workshop

For our mothers, who helped us find the song in
our hearts—DY and FS

For Liam, Addy, and Finn. The whole world is
your stage—JH

PENGUIN WORKSHOP
An Imprint of Penguin Random House LLC

Visit us online at www.penguinrandomhouse.com.

Library of Congress Cataloging-in-Publication Data is available upon request.

ISBN 9781524786502 (paperback)   10 9 8 7 6 5 4 3 2 1
ISBN 9781524786519 (library binding)   10 9 8 7 6 5 4 3 2 1

Contents

Where Is Broadway?

"Five minutes to curtain!" shouts the stage manager.

In the dressing rooms, the actors take their last looks in mirrors ringed with lights. They check their makeup, making sure their wigs are in place and their mics hidden. A singer does her final vocal warm-up, belting loudly. Her voice rings through the halls above the theater.

Other actors are going over their lines. There's a *tip-tap-clack* of tap shoes. It's the members of the chorus. They are all dressed in matching costumes, ready for the opening number. The costume designer quickly snips a thread off of the leading man's suit jacket. She straightens his hat and pushes him to his place on the stage.

Beyond the heavy red curtain, the audience settles into their seats, excited for what they're about to see.

The lights in the theater dim, and the conductor raises her baton. The orchestra begins the first notes of the overture (a sampling of the songs), and the curtain rises. This is Broadway. It's showtime!

The excitement happens over and over again, eight times a week—six nighttime performances and two in the afternoon, called matinees.

Everyone who works to make a show happen, from actors to producers, directors to designers, comes together to put on musicals, comedies, and dramas for audiences in theaters in the famous Times Square area of New York City. Some shows will become huge hits, like *Wicked* or *Hamilton* or *The Lion King*. And some will not even make it past their opening nights! This is the thrill, and sometimes terror (forgotten lines, falling scenery), of live theater. But this is Broadway, and there is nothing like it!

CHAPTER 1
A Long Path

Broadway is a very long, very busy street that runs north to south through the middle of Manhattan in New York City.

But Broadway is much more than just a street! It represents the history of American theater from its earliest days to the present. It reflects the hopes and dreams of people all across the country who want to make it big on the stage. It is where people from around the world come to experience the wonder of live theater.

Today, the heart of Broadway is around Times Square in midtown Manhattan. It's called the Theater District. But long before the Times Square theaters were built, long before there were flashing lights and giant billboards for shows, Broadway was important in a very different way. It is a part of the history of New York City.

The Lenape first inhabited the island of Manhattan. They named it Mannahatta which means "island of many hills." Most of the land was swamp and rock and not good for farming. The Lenape did not consider the island to be very important. Its main road was called the Wickquasgeck Trail.

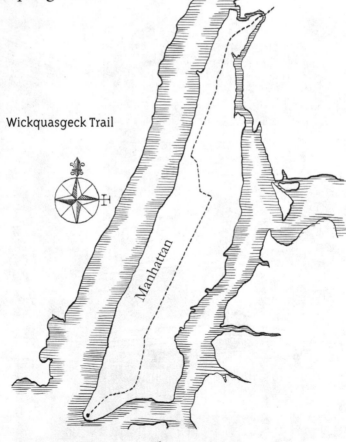

Wickquasgeck Trail

Manhattan

In the early 1600s, Dutch settlers established a colony on the tip of Manhattan. On May 24, 1626, they purchased the entire island from the Lenape, trading tools and other goods. Today the sum would be worth only about twenty-four dollars.

The Dutch named the trail Breede Wegh (or "broad road"). In 1664, the English captured the island. They named it New York, in honor of a famous duke, and they changed Breede Wegh to Broadway.

Theaters

In his play *As You Like It*, William Shakespeare wrote the famous line "all the world's a stage," and this is very true for theater productions! Shakespeare had his own theater, called the Globe, built in London in 1599. Before this, many shows had been performed in private homes or inns.

Long before that, the ancient Greeks and Romans performed plays in amphitheaters. An amphitheater is usually a circular or oval structure with bench-like seating, open to the air. The Colosseum in Rome is the largest amphitheater ever built and could hold between fifty thousand and eighty thousand people! It was sometimes used for plays, but mostly the Colosseum was used for huge spectacles like gladiator fights. Sometimes, the Romans would flood the Colosseum for battles at sea!

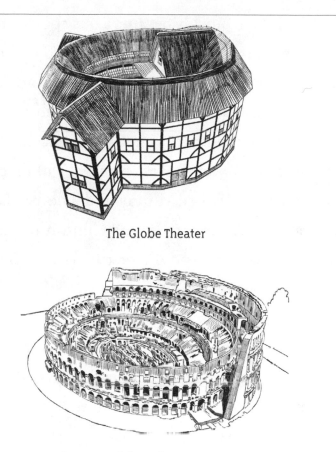

The Globe Theater

The ruins of the Colosseum in Rome

Most modern theaters are indoor spaces where the audience sits in front of a stage that has a "picture frame" around it.

Manhattan quickly became a busy port. Sailing ships with costly goods aboard came to and from the harbor. However, there was not much to do for entertainment. Both the Dutch and the English were Protestant. Their religion considered theater to be sinful. It wasn't until 1750 that two British actors, Walter Murray and Thomas Kean, appealed to Governor George Clinton to permit acting. He agreed, and the first New York theater opened.

Named the Nassau Street Theatre, it was at the southern tip of the island, just a few steps from Broadway. The theater held nearly three hundred people. Unlike the velvet seats in today's theaters, hard benches were the only places to sit. The light came from candles. It was so cold inside that the audience would bring bins of hot charcoal to stay warm. Nonetheless, people returned each night to see the lighthearted British comedies performed there. And soon, other acting troupes arrived.

"Give My Regards to Broadway"

The name Broadway appears in so many songs. One of the most famous, "Give My Regards to Broadway," comes from a Broadway musical. The song gained much greater popularity when it was sung in a movie called *Yankee Doodle Dandy*. The famous lines of the song are, "Give my regards to Broadway, remember me to Herald Square. Tell all the gang at Forty-Second Street, that I will soon be there!"

The next great downtown theater near Broadway was the John Street Theatre, opened in 1767. It was impressive, with three floors and two thousand seats. Some historians call it "the birthplace of American theater." Performances of Shakespeare's plays were especially popular.

Scene from *Romeo and Juliet*

When the American Revolutionary War began, most men were called to fight. People weren't going to see plays. After the colonists won independence, the new government outlawed what they considered "extravagant" British entertainments. Theater was once again forbidden.

The residents of Manhattan were already theater fans, so after the war, it didn't take very long for plays to resume. In 1798, the Park Theatre opened a block away from Broadway. For the first few years, the theater did not make much money and almost went out of business. But in 1808, a man named Stephen Price became the new manager. The theater was renovated to suit upper-class patrons. In addition, Price hired famous European actors and actresses. Price could charge more for tickets to performances with well-known stars.

As Manhattan continued to develop, the

wealthy class began to move a little farther north. New fancy theaters sprang up in these neighborhoods. The Bowery Theatre opened in 1826, and the luxurious Astor Place Opera House opened in 1847. Patrons had to dress in suits and gowns. They sat in plush seats that were reserved in advance.

The working class was not allowed in the new theaters, and they resented it. There was a growing tension between rich and poor in Manhattan.

In March 1849, a group of working-class men stormed the Astor Place Opera House because a British actor, William Charles Macready, was playing the starring role in Shakespeare's *Macbeth*. The rioters were angry that a popular American actor, Edwin Forrest, was not given the part.

Times Square

Times Square, originally developed in the 1880s as Long Acre Square, has seen many changes over the years. It was just after the city created Times Square in 1904 that electricity began lighting up theaters and their billboards, and it made the area a go-to place for many. It was during this time that the Interborough Rapid Transit Company (IRT), New York City's first subway system, was created, allowing New Yorkers a new way to travel.

Forrest championed an American style of performing Shakespearean plays. He acted with less flourish and fewer grand gestures than Macready. Forrest made his characters seem more like real people whom everyday working Americans could relate to. The "Astor Place Riot," also known as the "Shakespeare Riots," left more than twenty people dead.

Area near Forty-Second Street, 1830s

As New York City's population grew, local officials encouraged people to "move uptown and enjoy the pure, clean air." In 1836, a major road—Forty-Second Street—officially opened. It cut across Broadway. A new neighborhood was born.

By the 1870s, the area was the center of popular theater in New York City. A wealthy businessman named Oscar Hammerstein built the stately Olympia Theatre at Forty-Fourth Street in 1895 and the Victoria Theatre in 1899. (The Victoria was sold only sixteen years later, however, and became the Rialto Theatre, one of New York City's first to show a new kind of entertainment: movies!)

Other large theaters began opening as well, which looked very much like the Broadway theaters we go to today. In January 1905, the *New York Times* newspaper moved into a new building on West Forty-Third Street. From this time on, the whole area became known as Times Square.

The Great White Way

"The Great White Way" is a nickname for a large portion of the Broadway theater district, from Forty-Second Street to Fifty-Third Street. This area of New York City got this name because it was one of the first electrically lit streets in America. As early as 1910, many of the theaters on Broadway had dazzling electric marquees. In 1927, the journalist Will Irwin wrote, "Mildly insane by day, the square goes divinely mad by night. For then on every wall, above every cornice, in every nook and cranny, blossom and dance the electric advertising signs. . . . All other American cities imitate them, but none gets this massed effect of tremendous jazz interpreted in light."

CHAPTER 2
Separate Stages

Although slavery was abolished—ended—in New York State in 1827, African Americans continued to be treated as second-class citizens. Just one example of this was that they were not permitted in most theaters. So black people started their own.

In 1821, the first African American theater company, named the African Company, was founded by William Henry Brown. Brown was originally from the West Indies. Unlike others brought from his homeland as slaves, Brown had worked as a steward on a boat. His voyages took him to many places, including England and New York, where he fell in love with theater. His dream was to write and act in plays, and when he retired

he decided to do just that.

At that time in the United States, there were no acting roles for African Americans and no theaters for them to perform in. So William Henry Brown opened the African Grove Theatre as a place for his African Company to perform. Their first production was Shakespeare's *Richard III*, a play about a ruthless king's rise to power.

William Henry Brown is also considered to be the first African American playwright. He wrote and directed a play for the African Company called *The Drama of King Shotaway*. The play is about a war that happened in 1795–1796 in which black people from Caribbean islands fought English colonists.

One of the members of the African Company was a man named James Hewlett. Hewlett used

to sneak into the Park Theatre. From the very back of the balcony, he would watch classic plays performed by white actors. He carefully studied the way the actors moved and spoke, and he taught himself how

James Hewlett as Richard III

to perform the same way. Hewlett became a star at the African Grove Theatre and is known as the first African American Shakespearean actor.

Not many people took Brown's African Company seriously in the beginning. But as word spread about how impressive their shows were, the crowds grew and began to include white patrons as well. Owners of other theaters, like the Park Theatre, saw Brown and his company as competition. They began paying people to disrupt performances at the African Grove Theatre. They sent the police to shut down the theater several times. They even asked a judge to forbid the performance of Shakespeare's plays by the African Company. In 1823, the African Grove Theatre was forced to close for good.

For most of the nineteenth century, the only depiction of African Americans onstage was in racist minstrel shows. White actors would paint their faces black and perform songs and skits that mocked black people based on stereotypes. One of the popular characters in these plays was Jim Crow, a foolish, clumsy slave who sang and danced for his master's amusement. The role was so well known that late-nineteenth century laws separating black and white people became known as the "Jim Crow laws." Minstrel shows mostly disappeared by the 1920s, but elements of this cruel entertainment remained into the 1970s.

It was not until after the Civil War that black theater in New York City reemerged. African American theater at the end of the nineteenth and beginning of the twentieth centuries featured a new type of music, called "ragtime." Ragtime gets its name for the irregular "ragged" beat of the music. A black composer and performer named Scott Joplin gained worldwide fame as the "king of ragtime." In 1903, the first full-length all-black musical, *In Dahomey*, about a small country in Africa, opened on Broadway near Times Square.

It starred Bert Williams and George Walker, two well-known African American comedians of the era. The show ran for fifty-three performances, which was considered a big success at that time. It also had a long-running tour in cities across the United States.

Scott Joplin

In 1921, the ragtime musical *Shuffle Along*, by black musicians Eubie Blake and Noble Sissle, opened on Broadway. The show's success proved that audiences would come to see African American talent.

American theaters today embrace diversity, with black actors playing many roles that were historically portrayed by white actors. Plays and musicals are rightly cast based on talent rather than color.

Perhaps the best example of this is the Broadway musical sensation *Hamilton*, written by a Latin American artist named Lin-Manuel Miranda, who also starred in the title role when it opened on Broadway. America's other founding fathers, including George Washington and Thomas Jefferson, are portrayed by actors of color.

Scene from *Shuffle Along*

The story of Alexander Hamilton's rise from a penniless immigrant to a member of the Constitutional Convention and the first secretary of the treasury is told through rap and hip-hop. By having Hamilton portrayed by a person of color, his struggle to achieve respect and success takes on a deeper meaning. The determination of the many pioneers of black theater in America is expressed out loud when Hamilton sings, "I am not throwing away my shot!"

CHAPTER 3
The Dawn of the American Musical

Before the twentieth century, there were three types of theatrical performances with music. The first was opera. Operas were written in Europe (and eventually in America, but not until much later).

Operas were long and dramatic. They were almost always sung completely through, with no spoken dialogue. The plots were usually based on classic mythology or historic events. Opera was considered cultured, something for the wealthy class. Sadly, it still is today, although modern companies, like New York City's Metropolitan Opera, have been making successful efforts to bring in younger audiences.

There was also operetta, which was basically a short, lighthearted opera. Plots often portrayed love at first sight, swashbuckling adventure, and mistaken identities. The melodies were usually very bright and catchy, with fast-paced, satirical lyrics to match. Operettas were popular in New York City among all social classes. Most were written and produced first in England. The most famous were by W. S. Gilbert and Arthur Sullivan. Their most notable shows include *H.M.S. Pinafore* (1878) and *The Pirates of Penzance* (1879).

Scene from *The Pirates of Penzance*

Finally, the most popular type of musical theater in nineteenth-century America and into the twentieth was vaudeville (say: VAW-duh-vill). Vaudeville didn't have a plot like operas and operettas. Instead, vaudeville was a mix of songs, dances, and short comic sketches. Sometimes the shows had acrobats and animals performing tricks. In other words, something for everyone!

Originally, vaudeville was often performed in saloons for crowds of rowdy men. But a man named Tony Pastor, called the "father of vaudeville," decided to move this kind of show to larger stages to attract a middle-class crowd. In 1881, he opened the Fourteenth Street Theatre, the first of its kind created for vaudeville. Some performers, like Charlie Chaplin and Buster Keaton, later became silent-movie stars because of their knack for physical comedy.

In 1907, a man named Florenz Ziegfeld Jr. staged a show called the *Ziegfeld Follies*. Ziegfeld's

Charlie Chaplin and Buster Keaton

vision was to create a more glamorous, high-class version of vaudeville. His inspiration was a famous show from Paris called the Folies Bergère. The *Ziegfeld Follies* was a hit, so he created a new show almost every year until he died in 1932! The *Ziegfeld Follies* became known for its lavish productions with huge casts and elaborate scenery.

The famous "Ziegfeld Girls" danced with giant headdresses and enormous feather fans. Many actors, dancers, and composers got their big break working for the *Ziegfeld Follies*, including singer-comedian Fanny Brice and comedian W. C. Fields.

One of the composers was named Jerome Kern. He was the son of a Jewish immigrant from Germany. Kern had been working as a piano player for music publishers. He teamed up with

The *Ziegfeld Follies*

Oscar Hammerstein II (the son of theater owner Oscar Hammerstein). Together, they created a totally new kind of musical theater experience. Not opera. Not operetta. Not vaudeville. Instead, they created the first musical—a show in which all the music and singing are used to develop the characters and advance the plot. It was called *Show Boat*, following the lives of performers and stagehands on a Mississippi River showboat.

Although *Show Boat* is classified as a musical comedy, the story deals with some serious issues,

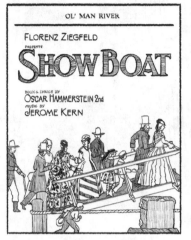

including race. It is also one of the first musicals to feature white and black actors together in one play. Though it was much different from the *Follies*, Florenz Ziegfeld was excited by the project and became its producer. The show opened in 1927. New York critics and audiences raved, and the show had 572 performances, which was a long run at the time.

In 1935, not long after *Show Boat*, another groundbreaking musical opened on Broadway. *Porgy and Bess* was written in an operatic sung-through style but brought together elements of jazz and African American folk music. A well-known white composer, George Gershwin, was the creator. The show had an almost entirely black cast and tells the story of a disabled man in love with a woman who wants to leave the South Carolina slum where they live. Although audiences at the time found it too slow and depressing, it is hailed by many critics as a musical masterpiece of the twentieth century.

Porgy and Bess

Richard Rodgers and Oscar Hammerstein II

Composer Richard Rodgers and lyricist Oscar Hammerstein II are considered the most famous musical-theater team in American history. In 1943, they took Broadway by storm with *Oklahoma!* It was a love story set in the early 1900s, when Oklahoma was a vast frontier and not yet a state. At the time the show opened, the country was fighting in World War II. The tragic bombing of US ships at Pearl Harbor had occurred only sixteen months before. *Oklahoma!* made Americans feel optimistic and proud of their country.

Scene from *Oklahoma!*

Dim Out

During World War II, the governor of New York said that a "dim out" was to take place to protect people as well as landmarks from being seen by enemy submarines in the waters around New York City. Traffic lights were even fitted with "blackout masks" so as not to be seen. The New York Times Building, called the Times Tower, had to dim its lights, including its dazzling electric news sign. And, of course, all the brightly lit theater marquees and signs in the Times Square area were dimmed to save electricity during the war.

Rodgers and Hammerstein went on to write some of the greatest musicals of all time, including *The Sound of Music* and *The King and I*. Although their shows were known for their memorable songs, many pushed boundaries in terms of

The King and I

subject matter and character development. In *Carousel*, the main character is a carnival barker named Billy Bigelow. In one song, which is over seven minutes long, Billy imagines what it will be like to be a father and decides to commit a robbery in order to provide for his soon-to-be family.

South Pacific, another classic from the team, is set during World War II on an island in the South Pacific Ocean. The show deals with the cultural divisions that existed between the American army and the native peoples. Rodgers and Hammerstein not only made their mark on musical history, but inspired many future composers and lyricists. Today, many theater historians and fans consider this the golden age of the American musical.

CHAPTER 4
Serious Drama

Original nonmusical plays, often referred to in theater as "straight plays," had been performed on Broadway for years. Popular melodramas offered emotional plots and larger-than-life performances. Although plays differed, they always had the same "stock characters"—the damsel in distress, the hero, and, of course, the villain.

It wasn't until the early to mid-twentieth century that American playwrights turned drama into something serious and wildly creative. Their plays showed how modern Americans struggled with their families, with work, with their senses of identity.

In the summer of 1915, a group of playwrights and other artists from New York City traveled to the tip of Cape Cod in Massachusetts. There they created a company called the Provincetown Players. The goal was to write about the true experiences of ordinary Americans, including their personal stories. Many of these plays were written in a style called realism. As the name suggests, these artists aimed to create characters and stories that reflected real life.

Playhouse of the Provincetown Players

Perhaps the greatest playwright to emerge from this group was Eugene O'Neill. O'Neill came from a theater family. He was born in a hotel room while his actor father was performing onstage. As a young man, he wandered from job to job, as far as England, Honduras, and Argentina. He suffered from depression and alcoholism. Dramas such as *Desire under the Elms* and *The Iceman Cometh* aimed to show that life could be harsh, disappointing, and even destructive.

Eugene O'Neill

His most famous play, *A Long Day's Journey into Night*, which premiered on Broadway in 1956, was about his own family. The characters include his father, a former headline actor who has become an angry drunk, and his mother, a drug addict. The play was so personal to him that he refused to have it produced until after his death. Lonely and angry, O'Neill died as he was born, in a hotel room.

Another member of the Provincetown Players was a writer named Susan Glaspell. Her play *Trifles*, written in 1916, tells the story of a wife who kills her abusive husband. Two men investigating his death cannot determine the cause, but the two women along with them put the pieces together. They decide to hide the evidence they've found and keep her secret. At that time, four years before women even had the right to vote, the play was highly controversial. It is still considered to be one of the most important plays of that century.

Eventually realism onstage began to change. The aim of a new generation of writers was to experiment with the way a play presents a story. *Our Town*, written in 1938 by Thornton Wilder, is set on a bare stage. A character known as the Stage Manager talks to the audience, narrating the story of a small town that could be anywhere in America. By leaving out scenery and props, the play was meant to be something that most Americans could relate to. *Our Town* is still frequently performed to this day.

Our Town

American playwrights continued to stretch the form of modern drama during the 1940s and 1950s, during and after the years of World War II. The most gifted include Arthur Miller, Tennessee Williams, and Lorraine Hansberry. All three wrote about the struggle of everyday Americans to find real meaning in their lives. Miller's greatest works, such as *Death of a Salesman*, portray the so-called American dream—owning a home, having a family, earning good money—as an empty fantasy.

Death of a Salesman, 1949

Tennessee Williams, a gay playwright, wrote characters in *The Glass Menagerie* and *A Streetcar Named Desire* who were, like himself, outcasts of society trying (and failing) to escape reality. *The Glass Menagerie* is the dreamlike memory of a poet named Tom, who is desperate to escape a world in which he feels trapped by his mother, Amanda, and an extremely shy, disabled sister, Laura. The

play's title comes from the set of tiny glass animals that are precious to Laura. Amanda forces Tom to find a husband for Laura, but the meeting is a disaster, and Tom leaves his family forever in search of happiness that he never finds.

Tennessee Williams

Lorraine Hansberry was one of the very few African American women whose writing was recognized in her time. Hansberry's most famous play is *A Raisin in the Sun*, which debuted on Broadway in 1959. It portrays the hardships of a black family living in a city, striving for more with the odds stacked against them. The Younger family is waiting for $10,000 from a life insurance policy after the death of their father. But one by one, their plans and dreams are crushed. There is a hopeful note at the play's end, however, that the family may perhaps move forward by holding on to one another.

Lorraine Hansberry

Drama at the end of the twentieth century often mixed comedy and tragedy together, much like real life does. An African American playwright named August Wilson wrote a collection of plays called *The Pittsburgh Cycle*. The cycle depicts the same black family during each decade of the twentieth century. Another groundbreaking play, *Angels in America* by Tony Kushner, is a two-part, eight-hour tragicomedy. Set in New York City in the 1980s, it takes place during the AIDS epidemic, when hundreds of thousands of gay men were dying.

Today, many talented voices showcase American drama. Playwrights such as Suzan-Lori Parks, Kenneth Lonergan, Stephen Karam, and Sarah Ruhl are pushing the boundaries in subject and style. They hold a mirror up to the challenges and achievements of life in the twenty-first century.

Angels in America

CHAPTER 5
Behind the Scenes:
"Putting It Together"

To an audience, a great play often looks like it magically came together with no effort at all. In reality, many people with different talents have worked together, often for years, to create the production an audience is watching.

A new show begins with the playwright, or sometimes a group of writers, who completes a script. It changes a lot from the first draft to the version that is performed on Broadway. The script can be a brand-new story, or it can be based on an old story, legend, or fable. Sometimes the script is adapted from a book or a movie. If the show is a musical, the playwright will work with a composer who writes the music and a lyricist who adds words to the music. Some composers write their own lyrics.

The next step is for the creators to find someone who will help them take their idea and make it into a show. It costs a lot of money to put on a professional play. Broadway shows are especially expensive. Today, most shows cost between $5 million and $25 million to produce! The person who takes care of the business side of a show is called a producer. The producer provides money of their own and asks others to invest money in the production as well. These investors are often called "angels." Big Broadway shows usually have more than one producer. The producer finds a theater where the show will be performed and is involved in hiring, and sometimes firing, the many people who will put the production together.

The most important person a producer hires is the director. The director transforms the play from the page to the stage. For a brand-new show, the director often works closely with the playwright, composer, and lyricist to bring their ideas to life. A director has to picture what the show will look like when it is eventually performed onstage. Directors oversee all the decisions for a show.

The director is responsible for casting the actors and guiding them through rehearsals. The director even figures out where the actors stand and move on the stage. This is called "blocking." Directors also work closely with the people who design the show's scenery, costumes, and lighting to make sure everything is the way the director thinks it should be. Rehearsals usually take place in a studio or performance space and then, shortly before opening, move to the Broadway theater that has been booked for the show.

Waiting in the Wings

When the leading man twists his ankle doing a spin or the starring lady loses her voice hitting the high note, someone has to take their places. The understudy is the performer who rehearses a role, or sometimes roles, in case they have to take the regular performer's place. That means they have to memorize all the lines, singing, and dancing for the part they are understudying for and be ready to take over at a moment's notice. Sometimes they are members of the chorus, but occasionally they simply  wait backstage (or "in the wings") in case they are needed. Some now-famous understudies who became stars include Taye Diggs, Sutton Foster, and Matthew Morrison. After all, the show must go on!

Sutton Foster

The dancing in a show is created by a choreographer. A choreographer works with the cast to help create all the dance numbers. This often starts in a small studio—not the theater— with just a piano or a recording of the music. As the numbers are mastered, the costumes and footwear are added, so that the performers will know how to move in what they will be wearing onstage.

Bob Fosse (1927–1987)

Sometimes, the choreography of a show is as important as the stage direction itself. Bob Fosse was a legendary choreographer who created his own style of dancing that is famous to this day. This style is sometimes referred to as the "Fosse amoeba." The dancing often includes sideways shuffles, rolled shoulders, turned-in knees, and the ever-famous "jazz hands." Much of Fosse's choreography has actors in top hats and gloves, signatures of the

Fosse look. Bob Fosse won many awards in his lifetime, including multiple Tony Awards (for Broadway shows), Emmy Awards (for TV shows), and Oscars for his work in film.

Of course, it takes many more people to make a show! Makeup artists, stagehands, the orchestra, dressers (people in the wings of the stage who actually help actors get dressed in "quick-change" scenes), and so many more all make the show that audiences see once the curtain rises.

CHAPTER 6
The Thoroughly Modern Musical

Over the years, Broadway musicals have changed in many ways. As audiences grew and theater became more popular, the types of shows that were being created changed, too. While the stories of the young United States were told in shows like *Oklahoma!*, new voices were rising that challenged this idealism in both form and content.

The show *Hair*, created by Gerome Ragni, James Rado, and Galt MacDermot, made its debut in 1967 at a theater in downtown Manhattan. Considered the first rock musical, the show was very different from what audiences were used to seeing in shows like *Oklahoma!* Written during the Vietnam War, *Hair* is about young hippies who look toward music and drugs to find escape and peace. At the time, this was very controversial.

The show was seen as "anti American" because it went against the values of conservative people who were for the war in Vietnam and against the idea of free love. In one scene, the cast is naked on the stage, something audiences definitely weren't used to! The first production of *Hair* ran for just six weeks and then, after more rehearsal and rewriting (often called a "workshop"), it reopened in a Manhattan dance club called Cheetah. There was only one rule from the owner of Cheetah: The show had to be over by 10:00 p.m. so that the dancing could begin! Then in April 1968, just after the nation grieved over the assassination of

Dr. Martin Luther King Jr., Broadway finally welcomed *Hair* to the Great White Way. It ran for 1,750 performances and has toured the United States—and the world—since that time.

A few years later, in July 1975, *A Chorus Line* opened on Broadway. This show, too, was a game changer. Standing in a line facing the audience, actors are supposed to be trying out to be in the chorus of a Broadway musical. The audience never learns the name of this show or what it's about, only that it will star a famous actress. The stage for the show was bare, as it often is when actors try out for shows. In *A Chorus Line*, they dance and sing out into a dark theater for "the director," a character who is heard but never seen by the audience.

THE DIVAS!

Broadway's history has been full of powerful leading ladies, both on and off the stage. These unforgettable actresses are Broadway's divas. *Diva* comes from the Latin word for goddess. Although the term sometimes brings to mind a demanding actress who storms off the stage during rehearsal, divas are best remembered because of their talent. Some were wide-eyed and optimistic, like Mary Martin, who won her first of four Tony Awards for Best Actress in *South Pacific*. Others became known as bold and brassy, like Ethel Merman, who brought down the house as Mama Rose

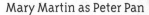

Mary Martin as Peter Pan

in *Gypsy* in 1960, and
Patti LuPone who did
it again in the same
role forty-eight years
later. Two divas even
shared the stage in
Wicked, when Idina
Menzel and Kristin

Patti LuPone as Evita

Chenoweth played the two witches of Oz. One thing
they all have in common, though, is the ability to
belt out a showstopping tune!

Idina Menzel and Kristin Chenoweth in *Wicked*

While auditioning, each actor tells about their life and what made them want to be in show business. In one scene, an actress sings "Nothing" about how her difficult experience in drama class made her want to be an actress even more.

A Chorus Line was nominated for twelve Tony Awards the year it opened on Broadway, and it helped to change the way people thought of what a musical could—and should—be. It ran for over six thousand performances and was the longest-running show in Broadway history until *Cats* came along.

During these years, a young composer and lyricist named Stephen Sondheim was cutting his teeth in musical theater. He got his start by writing the lyrics to shows such as *West Side Story* (1957), an updated version of *Romeo and Juliet* that takes place in Manhattan and follows the love of a white boy and a Puerto Rican girl.

Stephen Sondheim

After this initial success, Sondheim began to compose music as well. He hoped to create a different type of musical experience for the audience. Two of his most famous shows are *Into the Woods* and *Sweeney Todd*. In *Into the Woods*, Sondheim takes classic fairy tales like "Little Red Riding Hood," "Jack and the Beanstalk," and "Rapunzel" and weaves them into a dark musical story. In maybe his most famous show, *Sweeney Todd*, he tells the story of an angry barber who kills his patrons and bakes them into meat pies in Victorian London!

Sweeney Todd

Sondheim is considered a master of both lyrics and music—although critics have often said he can't write a "hummable tune."

The 1980s saw lots of big hits, especially must-see shows like *Cats* and *The Phantom of the Opera*. New York, London, and soon much of the world became entranced by these big, splashy productions. They were created by a composer named Andrew Lloyd Webber. He started out with *Jesus Christ Superstar*, which had great popularity portraying biblical characters in a rock-concert setting. He also wrote the show

Andrew Lloyd Webber

Evita, about the life of Eva Perón, the First Lady of Argentina from 1946 to 1952. But it was in 1982 that his musical *Cats*, based on poems by T.S. Eliot, premiered at the Winter Garden Theatre and became an international hit. The production didn't close until the year 2000! (And *Cats* had a successful Broadway revival in 2016–2017!)

The Phantom of the Opera opened on Broadway in 1988 and is still running. The story is about a mysterious man who lurks in the basement of the Paris opera house. The set is an amazing re-creation of an old Paris opera house. At one point, an enormous chandelier crashes onto the stage! There is also a scene in which the Phantom and Christine, his love interest, float across the stage in a boat! This is now the longest-running Broadway musical.

The Tony Awards

The Tony Awards are considered the Academy Awards of theater. The awards started in 1947. They range from Best Musical to Best Choreography, Best Performance by a Leading Actress in a Play to Best Costume Design of a Musical, and on and on. It wasn't until 1978 that the awards were shown on television. Since then, the ceremony has become a glamorous, showstopping evening, with many performances as well as the awards presentations. For the first two years of the awards, there was no actual Tony Award statue. The men got money clips, and the women were given makeup compacts.

Then there was a contest to design a special award memento. The winning design was a medallion with the famous masks of comedy and tragedy on one side, and on the other, a portrait of Antoinette Perry, the former leader of the American Theatre Wing, who was also an actress, director, and producer.

While the shows got splashier, Times Square grew seedier. The neighborhood had gotten steadily worse from the 1950s through the 1980s. It became one of the most dangerous areas in New York City. Then in 1990, the city government created a program to make Times Square a place where tourists and New Yorkers would be comfortable, safe, and happy. In 1995, the New Victory Theater opened as the first theater dedicated to children's shows. That was the beginning of the turnaround.

New Victory Theater

Now more than 355,000 people are on the streets of Times Square every day. The theaters have more than five thousand seats in use. From 2000 to 2015, the number of visitors to Times Square increased by 22.1 million.

As a sign of how hugely the area had changed, by the mid-1990s, Disney arrived on Broadway.

In 1994, its first Broadway musical, *Beauty and the Beast*, opened. It was a hit, followed by *The Lion King* in 1997. Disney took a big risk in *The Lion King* by hiring a relatively unknown director for the show. Her name was Julie Taymor, and  she brought the world of *The Lion King* to life in ways that had never before been imagined on a Broadway stage. Actors wore costumes that mimicked the movement of animals; some used beautifully handmade puppets to

Julie Taymor

depict the animal characters in the show. Truly, Broadway was a destination for families from all over the world!

Another historic musical of the '90s was *Rent*.
A young man named Jonathan Larson wrote
about what his life had been like in Manhattan's
East Village neighborhood. His plot was based on
a famous opera called *La Bohème*, about a group
of struggling artists in Paris in the 1800s. In
Rent, Larson addressed many taboo topics—lack

Original cast of *Rent*

of respect from the police, drug use, and HIV and AIDS. The show opened in January 1996 at a small theater in the East Village. Critics and theatergoers were captivated by the story and its creator. Before long, the show was set to move to the Nederlander Theatre for its Broadway debut.

However, the show's quick success also met with real-life tragedy. The night before *Rent* opened, Jonathan Larson, who was only thirty-five years old, died suddenly of a rare heart disease. The sadness of the sudden passing of such a gifted young artist has made *Rent*—and its unconventional story—a part of Broadway's history.

Jonathan Larson

Currently, the Broadway landscape is a wonderful combination of many different types of shows. Besides *Hamilton*, there's the box office–

breaking *Wicked*, the story of two witches in Oz who go from enemies to friends. And *Dear Evan Hansen*, a show about a boy with social-anxiety disorder that has resonated with so many theatergoers,

especially teenagers. It is clear that there will always be something for everyone on Broadway!

Lin-Manuel Miranda (1980–)

Many people became aware of a young singer, songwriter, and composer named Lin-Manuel Miranda when his first Broadway musical, *In the Heights*, premiered in 2008. It was based on his own experiences of growing up in a Latino neighborhood of New York City called Washington Heights. But it was in 2015 that he became an international superstar with his hit hip-hop musical *Hamilton*. He wrote the book (the story of the show), lyrics, and music for the show, and starred in the title role of Alexander Hamilton. In 2016, the show received the Pulitzer Prize in Drama and won eleven Tony Awards, including two for Lin-Manuel for Best Book and Best Original Score of a Musical. The original Broadway cast recording of *Hamilton* also went on to win the Grammy Award for Best Musical Theater Album in 2016.

CHAPTER 7
Broadway . . . and Beyond!

Even though people hear all the time about Broadway shows, there are actually only five theaters on the street named Broadway. But there are forty-one theaters in the Times Square district, and at one time in the early twentieth century, there were many more. There are other types of theaters called Off-Broadway theaters.

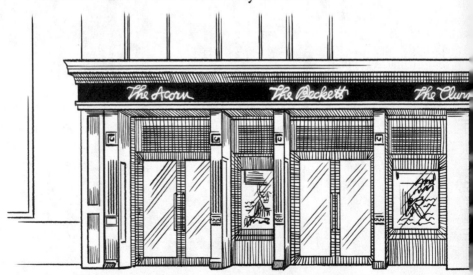

Theater Row in NYC puts on Off-Broadway
and Off-Off-Broadway shows.

What makes a show a Broadway show or an Off-Broadway show? It's not its location; it's the number of seats in the theater. If a theater has 499 seats or more, it's considered a Broadway theater. Having fewer than 499 seats makes it an Off-Broadway theater. And fewer than ninety-nine seats is considered an Off-Off-Broadway theater. But because the Tony Awards will only nominate shows that have a "Broadway" listing, many Off-Broadway shows will move to a Broadway theater if they are successful. Shows like *Little Shop of Horrors, Rent, Hair,* and *Hamilton* all began in smaller Off-Broadway theaters.

Better Nate Than Ever

In 2013, a Broadway actor and writer named Tim Federle published a book called *Better Nate Than Ever*, about Nate Foster, a thirteen-year-old boy with Broadway dreams. He devises a way to sneak out of his small town in Pennsylvania to go to New York City for *ET: The Musical* and get the part of ET! The book was so successful that it was followed by *Five, Six, Seven, Nate!* and *Nate Expectations*.

In the past two decades, a type of theater has become popular in which the audience, actors, and even the stage mix together. It is called "immersive" theater.

A show called *Sleep No More* was created in London and then moved to a large warehouse space in a Manhattan art-gallery district. It is based loosely on Shakespeare's *Macbeth*, about a Scottish general who murders to become king. The story that is told in *Sleep No More* is different for almost every member in the audience. Why? Because audience members don't sit and watch the production. Instead, they wear ghoulish white masks and are set free in the imaginary McKittrick Hotel, which is decorated in a run-down, spooky way. As the audience

wanders through room after room—bedrooms, hospitals, graveyards, an elaborate banquet hall, an abandoned apartment—they get glimpses of actors performing scenes, many with modern dance as a part of them, and the show unfolds around them. It is up to the audience members to follow the characters whose storylines are most interesting to them and to piece together the mysteries of the McKittrick Hotel.

In the original Broadway production of *Spring Awakening,* some audience members were seated on the stage and often were in the middle of some musical numbers. And before *Natasha, Pierre & the Great Comet of 1812* moved to Broadway, it was staged in a circus tent in Manhattan, where cast members sang and danced around the audience, sometimes even sitting at their tables, sharing a quick laugh—or bite of their food! The Broadway production was nominated for twelve Tony Awards in 2017 and won two.

Of course, Broadway shows aren't only staged in New York City. If a Broadway show becomes very popular, the producers often look to send the production with a different cast on a tour of other cities and sometimes throughout the world. This is a great way for more people who can't make a trip to New York City to see shows. Sometimes

if the show is very popular—like the jukebox musical *Jersey Boys*, about the doo-wop group Frankie Valli and the Four Seasons—the show's producers will start the tour while the show is still running on Broadway. (A jukebox musical is one in which most of the songs that are performed have been popular radio hits and the story of the show is written around the songs.)

Where else are Broadway shows produced? In schools throughout the country! The Junior Theater Festival, which takes place each spring in Atlanta, Georgia, is a way for Broadway producers to tell about new shows that are available to perform in schools. Students and teachers travel from all over the country to be part of the festival, which includes

workshops, performances, and sneak peeks of new shows. And, of course, performing in school plays has fueled dreams of becoming famous actors in countless kids. Sarah Jessica Parker, the well-known movie and television actress, played Annie on Broadway when she was just fourteen years old. This role launched her career, even though she never thought she would make it to Broadway after seeing Andrea McArdle, the original Annie. "[I] watched Andrea and assumed I would never be in *Annie*. I would certainly never play Annie, and I wouldn't be part of this sort of magical phenomenon that washed over Broadway," Sarah Jessica Parker said.

Sarah Jessica Parker

School productions are also important for producers and writers.

Why? Because schools have to pay fees to produce shows, and the writers and producers receive part of that money—this is called a licensing fee. Some shows help generate over $1 million or more a year in licensing revenue! In the last five years, *Annie* has been licensed more than thirteen thousand times to schools all around the world!

Glee

In 2009, the Fox Network premiered *Glee*, a show about a glee club in a school called William McKinley High. The show quickly became a huge success and helped make stars of Lea Michele (who had been in *Spring Awakening* on Broadway) and Chris Colfer. The show helped bring musical theater and performance even more into the mainstream for kids, much the way the movie and TV show *Fame* did in the 1980s.

Some producers have even created shorter versions of their biggest shows so that schools can produce them. And sometimes, more parts will be created in the "junior" version of the show so more students can perform. This idea was created by none other than Stephen Sondheim. He was worried about aging theater audiences and wanted his shows to have very long lives. He started with a school production of *Into the Woods*.

Student production of *Into the Woods*

PLAYBILL
Scranton Players
Scranton Middle School
Brighton, MI

Playbill—the magazine handed out to theatergoers as they reach their seats—has even taken part in this movement, providing software to schools to create their very own playbills for their shows!

With live theater, no two performances are exactly the same. An actor can forget their lines, a piece of scenery can get stuck, a light can burn out in the middle of a showstopping number. But the power of Broadway has remained the same. The cast and the audience come together to experience something very special. The power of a thrilling show is the reason why this art form has been around for centuries and will remain for centuries to come. Now it's possible for so many more to see shows all over the world and to feel firsthand how thrilling live performance can be!

Timeline of Broadway

1664 — British rename the Dutch "Breede Wegh" path as Broadway

1750 — Murray and Kean granted permission to open the Nassau Street Theatre

1821 — William Henry Brown founds the African Company

1849 — The Astor Place Riot takes place

1881 — The first vaudeville theater opens

1895 — Oscar Hammerstein opens the grand Olympia Theatre on Broadway

1903 — *In Dahomey* opens on Broadway

1907 — Florenz Ziegfeld Jr. presents the first of his *Ziegfeld Follies*

1916 — Susan Glaspell writes *Trifles* for the Provincetown Players

1927 — *Show Boat* premieres on Broadway

1935 — *Porgy and Bess* receives mixed reviews

1943 — Rodgers and Hammerstein's *Oklahoma!* premieres

1947 — The first Tony Awards are presented

1959 — *A Raisin in the Sun* by Lorraine Hansberry opens on Broadway

1967 — *Hair* debuts at the Public Theater

1988 — *The Phantom of the Opera* begins its record-setting run

1994 — Disney's first Broadway show, *Beauty and the Beast,* opens

2011 — *Sleep No More* premieres in Manhattan

2015 — *Hamilton* opens on Broadway

2018 — *The Band's Visit* wins ten Tony Awards, including Best Musical

Timeline of the World

1665	The Great Plague of London begins
1775	US postal system is established
1849	Elizabeth Blackwell becomes the first woman in the United States to earn a medical degree
1881	The Tuskegee Institute opens in Alabama
1896	The first modern Olympic games are held in Greece
1903	The Wright brothers fly their first airplane
1912	The RMS *Titanic* sinks on its first ever voyage
1914	World War I begins
1929	The Great Depression begins after the stock market crashes
1939	Nazis invade Poland; World War II begins
1947	Jackie Robinson becomes first African American to play in US major league baseball
1959	Fidel Castro comes to power in Cuba after revolution
1969	NASA sends the first humans to the moon
1985	The first *Live Aid* concerts are held in London and Philadelphia
1994	Nelson Mandela becomes the first black president of South Africa
2009	Barack Obama is sworn in as the first African American president of the United States
2016	Boxing icon Muhammad Ali dies
2018	France wins FIFA World Cup

Bibliography

Brantley, Ben. *Broadway Musicals: From the Pages of the New York Times*. New York: Abrams Books, 2012.

Charles River Editors. *Broadway: The History and Legacy of New York City's Theater Center and Cultural Heart*. Wauwatosa, WI: Charles River Editors, 2017.

Rendon, Jim. "Broadway Hits the Blackboard Circuit." *The New York Times*, February 25, 2018.

Riedel, Michael. *Razzle Dazzle: The Battle for Broadway*. New York: Simon & Schuster, 2015.

Viertel, Jack. *The Secret Life of the American Musical: How Broadway Shows Are Built*. New York: Sarah Crichton Books/FSG, 2016.

Websites

www.pbs.org/wnet/americanmasters/vaudeville-about-vaudeville/721/

www.blackpast.org/aah/african-company-african-grove-theatre

www.tonyawards.com/en_US/history/index.html

www.smithsonianmag.com/smart-news/choreographer-bob-fosse-forgotten-author-modern-musicals-180963746/

www.timessquarenyc.org/history-of-times-square

www.spotlightonbroadway.com/the-great-white-way-o